D0850729

the art of the nap

the art of the nap

HARRIET GRIFFEY

MQP

Published by **MQ Publications Limited**
12 The Ivories,
6–8 Northampton Street,
London N1 2HY
Tel: 44 (0) 20 7359 2244
Fax: 44 (0) 20 7359 1616
email: mail@mqpublications.com
website: www.mqpublications.com

Design by **Balley Design Associates**

ISBN: 1 84072 622 9

1 3 5 7 9 0 8 6 4 2

For David—with whom I'd
like to nap more often.

Printed and bound in China

*This book contains the opinions and ideas of the author.
It is intended to provide helpful and informative
material on the subjects addressed in this book and is
sold with the understanding that the author and
publisher are not engaged in rendering medical, health,
or any other kind of personal professional services in this
book. The reader should consult his or her medical, health,
or other competent professional before adopting any of
the suggestions in this book or drawing references from it.
The author and publisher disclaim all responsibility for
any liability, loss, or risk, personal or otherwise, which is
incurred as a consequence, directly or indirectly, of the use
and application of any of the contents of this book.*

Contents

1 The importance of the nap   **6**

2 Understanding sleep   **16**

3 Naps for all reasons   **48**

4 Nap necessities   **64**

NAPS SHOULD HAVE THE STATUS
OF DAILY EXERCISE....

Jane Brody

1

The importance of the nap

The history of the nap

The nap has a long and honorable tradition, and is ripe for reclamation. While we continue to recognize that napping is necessary for growing infants, who become uncooperative, grumpy, and tearful without it, we have forgotten that it can also be a useful and restorative tool for busy adults—especially those who become uncooperative, grumpy or tearful without it!

The twenty-first century is the 24-hour society realized. Modern technology and the global network mean that we are now required to disregard time zones, and our own internal clocks, to work faster and work more. Shift work, restricted in the past to certain careers and industries that provided a 24-hour service, has become the norm for many of us. Far from liberating us, internet technology has upped the ante: we are now expected to deliver immediately something that previously relied on time for completion before dispatch.

This apparent addiction to new technology is, however, at odds with the zeitgeist of the fledgling twenty-first century, with its emphasis on living in balance, in harmony with the natural world around us, in tune with our environment. As with many other examples of new ways of thinking and being, we need time to catch up, having been disorientated by the rapid pace of progress in the late 1980s and 1990s.

The art of the nap is absolutely in keeping with this zeitgeist of harmonious living, and is an antidote to the "me, me, me" attitudes of the past. It is about taking time, beginning with yourself but looking outward. It is this that will save us from the tyranny of global technology and the commercialism that drives it.

Our greatest resource in any achievement is our own ability, whether this is an intellectual, emotional, or physical ability. This ability needs nurturing through being used and also being allowed to rest. Overuse wears out the component parts of any piece of machinery, whereas judicious use extends its shelf life. There must be a work/life balance. The "time is money" mantra has overwhelmed the gentler wisdom that more, not less, can be accomplished if a little time is taken for oneself.

Obviously there are times when 100 percent effort is required for a period of time, but expended relentlessly it is counterproductive. Time out, it seems, is essential to both our bodies and our minds, and far from reducing what we can achieve, it extends the possibilities. In this way the nap becomes a strategy of resistance against global time. Not only that, it also increases our value, and by extension our self-worth, if we are not available every minute of the day!

UNLESS WE BEGIN WITH THE RIGHT ATTITUDE, WE WILL NEVER FIND THE RIGHT SOLUTION.

Chinese proverb

Polyphasic sleep

In contrast to sleeping in one block or phase, the term for which is monophasic sleep, polyphasic sleep is a pattern of sleeping in numerous phases throughout the twenty-four hours of the day. One of the benefits of this is, apparently, that regular sleep/wake cycles constantly refresh the brain and make it more productive. One proponent of this pattern was polymath Leonardo da Vinci, a stunningly impressive example of the benefits of polyphasic sleep.

Before the advent of the clock, polyphasic sleep patterns were much more the norm. You rose with the dawn and worked for a while. Then you ate and rested, and probably slept—especially as life was much more physically active for most people. Then you worked some more. And maybe invented the wheel. You followed your own rhythms, worked while you could, and slept when you couldn't. In the winter, before the advent of artificial light, there wasn't much else to do after dark but explore your thoughts, and sleep!

It is possible to train people to achieve polyphasic sleep patterns, and this is imposed on sailors when the night watch has to be covered, for example. Apparently, the United States military, which spends millions of dollars on sleep research, actively trains recruits in polyphasic sleep patterns. But what came naturally to our medieval ancestors now has to be learned.

Leonardo da Vinci

Leonardo da Vinci was said to sleep only an hour and a half a day, taking fifteen-minute naps every four hours. This may in part explain the phenomenal amount of work he achieved in his lifetime, not just in its execution but also in its range and sheer brilliance.

The cult of the siesta

In times of less hectic activity in chasing the dollar, having time to stand and stare was considered important. In many nineteenth-century paintings by Manet and Monet, Gauguin and Van Gogh, the siesta is depicted as a regular activity. Numerous examples of *Déjeuner sur l'herbe* exist in the art of the period, and they all depict the cult of the siesta. In addition, time out was valued not just for itself, but for the contribution it made to achievement. No one who did creative work toiled nonstop. Even those artists who claimed to sleep little would take naps.

The word "siesta" was introduced as a noun in Spanish in 1681, and has forever been associated with the Mediterranean lifestyle. The cult of the siesta remains more Mediterranean than Nordic, and it resists the Puritan work ethic. It is linked to the idea that man deserves a break in the middle of the day, having been up early and worked before it got hot. Late afternoon and early evening were also considered good times for activity, but the middle of the day—well, that was siesta time and not negotiable!

In 1825 Jean-Anthelme Brillat-Savarin wrote, "Man was not made to enjoy endless activity; Nature destined him for an interrupted existence." Just under 200 years later, we may tardily be starting to take note. Modern research has shown, through the analysis of road accidents, that we are at our least alert between 3a.m. and 6a.m., and 3p.m. and 6p.m. What better justification than this could there be for taking a siesta between the hours of 3p.m. to 6p.m?

THE SIESTA IS AN IMPERATIVE.

Thierry Paquot

Forty winks and the cat nap

These two descriptions give the sense that the nap doesn't last for long but is nevertheless effective. We all know how well cats can leap into action from apparently being fast asleep. The art or knack of napping is to do so in such a way that you don't sleep for too long, and you also avoid affecting your nighttime sleep and inadvertently causing insomnia.

People who nap during the day because they suffer from insomnia and sleep deprivation aren't really napping; they have a sleep disorder and sleep during the day because they can't stay awake and need to make up for lost sleep. Deliberate napping or daytime sleeping will make things worse. The nap isn't designed to compensate for lack of sleep, it's designed to reenergize you in order to enjoy the day more. You can't compensate for chronic sleep deprivation by napping; proper nighttime sleep patterns have to be reestablished even if, in the short term, napping seems to be the answer.

Those who sleep well at night, even for eight hours, can still benefit from a short nap. Napping isn't about making up for lost sleep, it's about refreshing the brain, wiping the cerebral slate clean to make room for fresh ideas and more efficient functioning. And if the brain is the HQ of bodily activity, then it isn't just the brain that benefits. Turning off the brain for a short break also turns off the control on some of the stress hormones, which reduces the load on other body systems.

Power napping

The current hot phrase for what has long been enjoyed by those nappers in the know is power napping. It seems there is very good evidence that burnout can be reduced, even avoided altogether, by the judicious use of napping. And if burnout concerns captains of industry, it's hardly surprising that their term for the solution includes the word "power!"

Burnout, it turns out, is more specific than just generalized fatigue. After a period of time working flat out, visual networks in the neural cortex of the brain begin to show signs of becoming saturated with information, through repeated use, and this eventually prevents further perceptual processing. You can go on looking, but that is as far as it's going to go! Which is no help at all in trying to get work done.

In 2002 research carried out at Harvard University took this idea further and conclusively proved a 20 percent improvement in the learning of a task involving hand/eye coordination after a nap. This reinforces what neurologists always knew and what we need to take note of: the brain needs time out and a nap is the perfect solution. But it's taking a while for this maxim to catch on.

Margaret Thatcher

While she was running the United Kingdom, Prime Minister Margaret Thatcher was renowned for sleeping very little—just four hours a night, it was claimed. However, she excelled at grabbing the occasional nap when she could, and pictures of her doing so are many. As one of the most effective twentieth-century leaders, whatever you thought of her politics, who ran the Government for seventeen years, she was obviously onto something!

Reclaim the nap!

Snatching a nap, being caught napping, snoozing, stealing forty winks—our very language suggests sleeping during the day is an illicit activity. But a survey carried out in 2000, which polled 1.2 million people in 251 countries, found that almost 25 percent of them napped regularly! What's more, researchers are finding that napping has beneficial effects on our productivity and long-term health. So don't let a napophobe persuade you that napping is a slothful activity. Nodding off doesn't mean losing out when it restores effectiveness.

For a nap to work best, it must last a minimum of ten minutes. Less than ten minutes, research shows, and the beneficial effect on performance lasts only an hour. If you want the benefit of a nap to get you through the rest of the day, opt for a minimum of twenty minutes and maximum of forty-five minutes. At the workplace, twenty to thirty minutes maximum would seem the most acceptable. You are making the nap work for its own sake, not as a catch-up for chronic sleep deprivation or a late night—although it will help here, too!

2

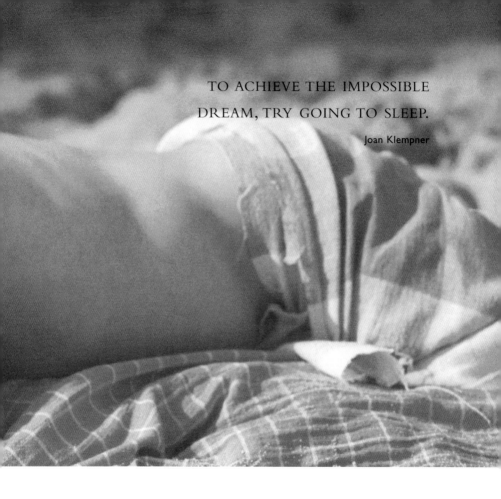

TO ACHIEVE THE IMPOSSIBLE
DREAM, TRY GOING TO SLEEP.

Joan Klempner

Understanding sleep

Circadian rhythms

We all have an internal body clock that functions on roughly a 24-hour cycle. This cycle is also referred to as a circadian rhythm, and it governs when you feel sleepy or wakeful, energized or tired, when you want to eat, and fluctuations in body temperature and hormone secretion.

In fact our natural circadian rhythm is closer to twenty-five hours than twenty-four hours, but we maintain the 24-hour cycle through a process of constant readjustment. Knowing how and when the fluctuations of our daily cycle occur, means that we can work with them rather than against them. For example, there is a natural energy surge in the morning, which peaks at around 11a.m. It then dips at around 3p.m., roughly eight hours after a 7a.m. waking and approximately halfway through a day's activity. For many people, this is the optimum time for a nap, to recharge for the remainder of the day, and to guard against extreme exhaustion before bedtime. Going to bed without feeling exhausted actually helps you sleep better: it allows time to relax, switch off and achieve better sleep!

These bodily rhythms are partly learned, which is why we can change them, or adjust to different time zones. But we are diurnal creatures, as opposed to nocturnal, meaning that we are geared to function during daylight hours and sleep when it is dark. This process is influenced most by the hormone melatonin, secreted by the pineal gland. It is the secretion of melatonin, which is a derivative of serotonin, a hormone responsible for influencing mood, that maintains our day and night patterns. The secretion of melatonin increases in response to the reduced light at night, helping us to sleep, and it can be taken in pill form to help induce sleep in people who suffer from insomnia. We know that the secretion of this hormone decreases as we age, hence elderly people often find it difficult to sleep well and soundly at night, and are more prone to napping during the day to compensate.

Hormone secretions also control temperature fluctuation. For example, your temperature begins to drop toward its daily minimum as you fall asleep at the end of the day, and begins to peak again as you wake. Levels of corticosteroids diminish toward the end of the day, then build to a high level just before you wake. This explains why you feel the cold when you get very tired and how, as a result of inadequate amounts of sleep, you can overproduce "awake" hormones to compensate. In order to maintain well-functioning circadian rhythms, what our bodies really like is regularity.

Sleep cycles

We don't just fall asleep and stay solidly asleep for six, seven, or eight hours. We actually sleep in cycles of changing brain activity, and while our bodies can manage physically with little or no sleep over a period of time, our brains just can't. Switching off conscious brain activity, through sleep, is essential for brain health and proper functioning.

The two distinct phases of sleep are called REM (rapid eye movement) and non-REM sleep, and we move in and out of these phases through the four stages of sleep. Stage 1 is a drowsy state, where we remain aware of what is going on but sleep becomes irresistible . We move to Stage 2, where we are actually falling asleep, but where it is also possible to wake easily. Then we move through Stage 3 to the deepest sleep of Stage 4, sometimes referred to as "deep wave" sleep. This is because an EEG (electro-encephalogram) scan shows deeper and longer brainwaves, compared to the shorter, faster brainwaves of lighter sleep. During Stage 4 sleep, breathing and heart rate become very stable, and slower. It's very difficult to wake during this stage of sleep, although a smoke detector alarm, or baby's cry, would probably do it as the brain is still able to process information.

A complete sleep cycle, passing through these four stages, takes around ninety minutes and consists also of non-REM sleep interspersed by REM sleep. REM sleep accounts for around 20 percent of all sleep. Babies' sleep cycles last around fifty minutes, but the lapse between stages is shorter. They tend to fall into a deep sleep very quickly but have lighter periods of sleep more often.

Brainwave patterns show that REM sleep is closest to Stage 1 sleep in terms of brain activity, and it is when we dream. REM sleep is considered an active stage of sleep because of the brain activity, although physical activity is restricted, to avoid us literally acting out our dreams! Dreaming is, however, essential to our psychological wellbeing, whether or not we remember our dreams. It is the way in which our brains process emotional and other material, and is thought to play a part in the transfer of short-term memory to longer-term storage.

The importance of understanding sleep cycles, when it comes to napping, is that we can go from Stage I sleep to REM sleep but progress no further, and so wake refreshed after only twenty to thirty minutes. This is ideal for napping: it clears the head and relaxes the body but doesn't take you into the deeper sleep from which it is difficult to wake. The art of napping is to train your body and mind to do this and, although some find it tricky at first, it's worth the effort.

Albert Einstein

Another great brain, Albert Einstein developed the Theory of Relativity on very little nighttime sleep, but lots of naps. He was not someone who decried sleep, as did Thomas Edison, but needed a lot. However, he seemed to practice the art of polyphasic sleep, much as Leonardo da Vinci did before him.

A man's dreams are an index
to his greatness.

Zadok Rabinwitz

Brainwaves

An EEG, which stands for electro-encephalogram, measures the electrical activity of brainwaves, and these can be recorded over a period of time, showing how they fluctuate and change. We react all the time to visual, emotional, sensory, and auditory stimuli, and this can easily be seen in our waking brainwaves.

There are four types of brainwaves: alpha, beta, delta, and theta. Alpha is seen in wakefulness where there is a relaxed and effortless alertness. Beta is seen in highly stressful situations, and where there is difficult mental concentration and focus. Delta is seen only in the deepest stages of sleep (Stages 3 and 4). Theta is seen in light sleep and drowsiness (Stages 1 and 2) when we dream.

Each of the four types is good for something different. They function much like the different gears on a car. Delta (the slowest wave) is first gear, theta is second gear, alpha is third gear and beta is fourth gear. No single gear is best for

every driving situation, and no single brainwave is best for all of the challenges of life. However, many people "drive" their brains inappropriately, never accessing all four options, in particular theta and alpha waves. The consequences of remaining dependent on beta waves in this manner are low productivity and a high rate of illness.

Here is what can happen. We are woken from deep sleep (delta waves) by an alarm clock. We immediately feel stress and anxiety (beta waves). We haven't had enough sleep so we grab some coffee to create greater wakefulness and rush for the door (more beta waves) which suppresses any helpful theta or alpha waves. A stressful day working hard finds us continually relying on beta waves to get things done before we rush home and fall asleep exhausted, into delta waves.

This endless cycle and pattern of behavior is a missed opportunity: a lack of alpha waves in particular means very little creativity in our approach to life and the imaginative problem-solving that it often requires. Working toward more alpha waves means less anxiety, a much stronger immune system, and better physical and emotional wellbeing in line with these factors.

The art of napping is also the art of allowing alpha and theta brainwaves to complement beta and delta waves. Alpha waves especially are associated with bursts of creativity, inspiration, and peak performance.

Not only can time out, and taking a nap, help access these positive brainwaves, they can also help reintegrate the two hemispheres of the brain. The left side and the right side of the brain have different strengths, and synchronizing the two sides brings a balance to our rational and intuitive sides, making our thought processes more complete and potentially more effective. Being right- or left-brain dominant means working with only half the tools available to you, and therefore not working as well as you could. So learn to nap now!

Creativity often consists of merely turning up what is already there. Did you know that right and left shoes were thought up only a little more than a century ago?

Bernice Fitz-Gibbon

Meditation

Another way to produce lots of alpha waves is through meditation. Even better, in terms of accessing your brain's potential, is to use meditation to access theta waves, and the possibility of a state of altered awareness that is extremely relaxing and creative. Meditation used to be thought of as on the flaky side of Eastern mysticism, and made a lot of people suspicious. What we now know is that those who learn to meditate are really on to something—not least, allowing alpha waves to help them utilize their brain's power more adequately, while also reducing the effects of stress on both mind and body.

Meditation is not an alternative to a nap, but may be a precursor; like the art of napping it is a learned skill. It takes an initial practice of around ten to fifteen minutes a day, and as with a lot of skills, some people find it easier to master than others. For many, attending a weekend course of instruction, or a retreat, can often provide a good start but it's not essential. You can learn to meditate on your own.

Preparation for meditation includes getting comfortable and utilizing a calming pattern of breathing (see page 32). The idea is consciously to reduce your brain's activity and you do this by allowing any thought processes to simply come and go without examination.

This is not easy! We are so geared up to thinking about the next thing we have to do, even while doing something else, that our brains are constantly in a state of anticipation and this feels normal, as opposed to the alternative. Many people find that focusing on an object, such as a candle flame, working our way through the breathing and relaxation exercises in preparation, or repeating a phrase or word (a mantra) helps. Eventually, these unwelcome intrusions into our thoughts just fail to register, and we are meditating.

Relaxation

Ask people how they relax, and many will look at you blankly! Lack of relaxation is a common problem of the twenty-first century, which demands a resistance strategy for the sake of our health and wellbeing. Constant tension and stress causes physical problems, from raised blood pressure to irritable bowel syndrome. Our bodies feel the stress of the tension in our muscles, and it serves to makes us feel emotionally stressed, too. It's a vicious circle and it's insidious: it creeps up on us until living in a state of tension feels normal and changing down a gear is extremely difficult.

Muscular tension, which occurs automatically when we live in constant stress, has an inhibiting effect on relaxation. Sometimes it gets to a point where the muscular tension is so locked in that it becomes impossible to shift without external help, such as a massage. Bear this in mind, and try to avoid it happening by introducing some regular exercise to loosen up your muscles, and relaxation practices, into your daily life.

Tension in muscles restricts their blood flow and oxygen supply, so they have to function without an adequate energy supply, which makes them lax and susceptible to damage. The structures they are supposed to support, such as the neck, shoulders, and spine are also vulnerable to damage. Having to function without adequate oxygen also means that muscles produce lots of lactic acid. High levels of lactic acid constantly in the body place additional strain on the liver, which has to metabolize it. The liver converts lactic acid, or lactate, to glucose for energy—which contributes to the body's sense that it should be doing some physical exercise! Persistently high levels of lactic acid can also contribute to chronic fatigue syndrome. It's a vicious circle.

The nap

A regular daytime nap can go a long way to helping overcome the many stresses and strains of modern life, whether you are a high-flying executive, stay-at-home parent, or student. For many, actually napping is not going to be possible straight away as there will be a tendency to fall into too deep a sleep. Initally you have to remove some of the obstacles to relaxation; then you can move on to the art of napping.

Be reassured it's worth the effort. A nap enables you to take time out to recharge physically and emotionally and, as described above, it can be essential in both improving productivity and performance, and avoiding health problems.

Learning to nap

The art of napping takes practice. It requires a learned ability to be able to switch off from the concerns, demands, and stresses of daily life for a short period, to control the length of time you have switched off, and to wake refreshed. It is a skill that comes easier to some than to others, but practice does make perfect and learning it will prove invaluable.

The aim of napping is to achieve both Stage 1 and Stage 2 of sleep, plus a period of REM sleep, but no more. This can be achieved in twenty to thirty minutes, but any longer and you risk lapsing into deeper sleep that is difficult to wake from, and disruptive to your brainwaves. You need to train yourself to drop off but wake again within that period of time. For some people, it's worth setting a timer to go off at around twenty-five minutes. Just in case!

You also need to establish a pattern that is right for you and leads to a nap. You need an almost Pavlovian response to the idea of taking a nap, so you can learn to nap quickly and efficiently at will. Fortunately, there are techniques that will make dropping off easier and make the art of napping one of your life skills. Read on!

Breathing

We all breathe automatically, from the moment of birth until we die. But our breathing is also something we can influence at will, and because of this mind/body link we have a powerful tool at our fingertips. We can learn to breathe in a way that influences our physical, psychological, and spiritual wellbeing. Simply by breathing in a mindful, focused way, we can clear the head of other extraneous thoughts.

Most of us breathe very shallowly, using the top part of the chest. Inadvertently this creates tension in the chest that radiates up into our shoulders and the muscles of our neck, forehead, and face, and also restricts the internal organs of the abdomen. We tend to breathe as if we are in preparation for "flight or fight" and if this state of arousal becomes habitual, the tension in our bodies can't be relieved and stress hormones continue to exert their effect. It becomes a vicious circle.

The good news is that although we may breathe in this inadequate way, it is possible to learn to breathe from the diaphragm, which relieves tension and stress. We can also raise our internal oxygen levels by breathing properly. This will regenerate our cells and ourselves physically, reducing the lactic acid in muscles that makes them stiff and tense, and reducing the secretion of stress hormones, and imparting a feeling of relaxation. Breathing diaphragmatically, as our bodies are designed to do, also means that the diaphragm stops being a constricted ring around the aorta (that takes blood from the heart to the body), which should reduce blood pressure. It also allows the colon underneath to be gently massaged rather than constricted, which helps reduce a tense gut and its associated problems. According to many stress experts, learning to breathe properly is the most important step to take in the management of stress.

Breathing from the diaphragm

Lie on your back with knees bent, so your back is comfortably flat on the floor without strain.

Consciously relax your shoulders, and tuck your chin in so your neck is long. If it makes you more comfortable, slip a small cushion under your head. Gently rest one hand on your upper chest, and one on your abdomen.

Close your eyes and breathe in gently and regularly through the nose, and out through the mouth.

Notice your chest rising and, on each breath, take the air a little deeper into the abdomen so you can feel your ribs expand slightly, your diaphragm stretch, and your abdomen extend.

Place your hands by your sides and continue breathing in this way.

As your breathing becomes calmer and more efficient, you should find that you are naturally breathing in and out, between twelve and sixteen times a minute, even as you really relax.

Practice for ten minutes, two or three times a day, until this new way of breathing becomes automatic whether you are lying, sitting or standing.

Sometimes it's helpful to intone the word "in" silently on the in-breath, and "out" on the out-breath. It sounds obvious, but is actually quite helpful when trying to keep your mind focused on your breathing.

If this isn't enough to stop distracting thoughts crowding in, try thinking of yourself as a pebble, dropping into a pool of water, sinking down and down through the still, cool depths. This tactic is also known as visualization.

Visualization

Visualization is an upmarket term for imagining yourself somewhere where you feel safe, secure, and peaceful. Don't be discouraged if you find this quite hard at first—many people do, and it can take a lot of concentration to start with.

Imagine a place—maybe a lovely, warm, sandy beach where all you can hear is the gentle lapping of the waves. Or envisage a beautiful woodland walk where dappled sunlight creeps through the leaves overhead, the air is soft, and the only sounds are the occasional birdsong and the rustle of your footsteps on fallen leaves—choose whatever works for you.

Experience it, in your imagination and through your senses. Do you feel warm? Feel the sun's rays gently penetrating your clothes, and warming your skin. What are the sounds you can hear? Maybe birdsong. Maybe waves. Maybe running water. What can you see in your mind's eye? Is the light gentle, gloomy, or bright? Are there trees? Mountains? Lakes? By concentrating on imagined physical sensations as you take yourself through this visualized space, you free your conscious mind from the bombardment of other stimuli. You may even find you drift off for a few minutes! The nap is just the beginning.

Salvador Dali

Salvador Dali claimed to have given up conventional sleep, opting for regular dozes instead. He would sleep in a chair and hold marbles, or a spoon, in one hand, over a metal bowl. As soon as he fell asleep, the marbles or spoon would drop, clattering into the metal bowl, and the noise would wake him. This improvisation on normal sleep, and the effect it had on him, may partly explain the extraordinary nature of his paintings.

Letting go

The process of letting go of conscious thoughts, worries, and concerns is very hard for many people. It takes practice. There are some very good psychological reasons why we can become fixated on external concerns: for one, it takes our mind off other things that might worry us even more! Getting worked up about life becomes something we are accustomed to; it feels normal and we find it difficult to let it go. Understanding this, and understanding the necessity of letting go, even if only for short periods, is the first step toward achieving it. For some, learning a skill such as meditation, is the perfect answer.

MEDITATION IS A LITTLE DROP OF PERFUME
THAT SUFFUSES THE DAY WITH ITS GRACE.

R. D. Laing

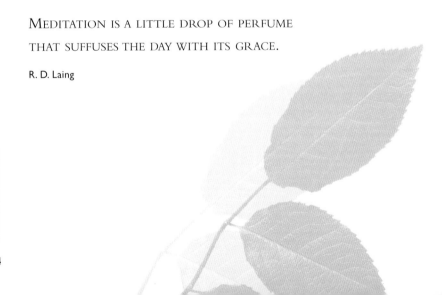

Banishing worries

If you are a natural-born worrier, letting go and banishing free-floating anxiety will be almost impossible at first. This is why breathing exercises and visualization are important: those of us who are worriers need an alternative for our brains to work on before we can wean ourselves off worrying! Breathing, relaxation, and visualization are all part of the process of learning to reduce the amount of time spent worrying—which seldom achieves much except increase beta brainwaves and exhaust the worrier.

Understanding how ineffective worrying is can also help reduce the hold it has on us. A stress expert once explained that worrying works as a sort of insurance. We think that if we worry about things they won't actually happen, because our actual experience is that the things we worry about seldom happen. We subconsciously actually manage to convince ourselves that worrying has this magical effect of stopping the bad things from happening. It's not true! What's more, it's a waste of time. Think of what you could be doing with all that energy you are currently putting into worrying about something that rationally, you know may not actually happen. If you are sure it will happen, worrying still won't help: try to channel your energy into finding a constructive solution to the problem rather than magnifying it with your anxiety.

Nap time is not an opportunity for a worry session, so practice all the techniques that help to shut out unwelcome thoughts—the perfect nap is within reach.

Worry never robs tomorrow of its sorrow, it only saps today of its joy.

Leo Buscaglia

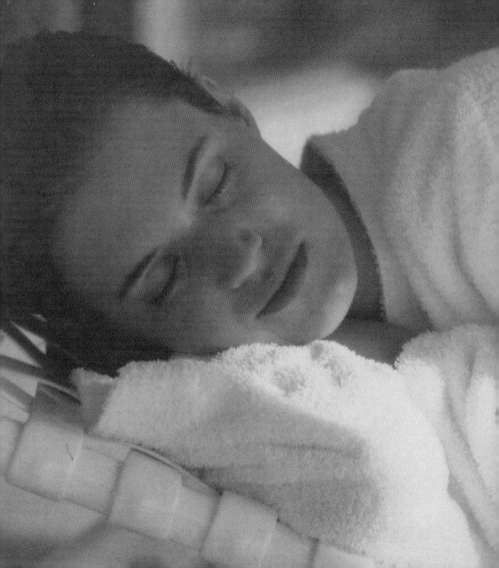

Resting the mind

If you have managed to calm your breathing, visualize a safe and pleasurable place, relaxed your body, let go, and banished worries, you will be able to rest your mind. And once your mind is at rest, you will nap and wake refreshed.

Take rest; a field that is rested gives a beautiful crop.

Ovid

Reversing morning burnout

You know the feeling. You hit the deck running and find yourself working flat out for six hours, accomplishing a lot. At this rate, you think, I will get that report completed by the end of the day. Suddenly the words cease to flow, and constant interruptions begin to irritate you. Someone asks if you'd like a sandwich and you snap their head off. What has happened? Burnout. How to alleviate it? Time out. A nap.

For most of us, the optimum time to nap is after lunch, before resuming our work or afternoon activities. This is partly because when we eat, in order to digest our meal, our blood supply is focused on the stomach, rather than the brain. Which is why we often feel sleepy after we've eaten. Once food is digested, the nutrients replenish our energy and we are ready to go again.

Early afternoon is also a good time for a nap, because it is normally about eight hours since we woke, and approximately halfway through our day. Even more important, it is beneficial to our ability to function for the rest of the day—that is why time out, in the form of a nap if possible, is so useful.

Research suggests that by the end of the morning, the first burst of energy after waking has generated a lot of productive activity, but to continue without a break creates burnout. This is both counterproductive in the short term and damaging to health in the long term.

Finding the time that works for you

Whether you work at home or in an office, whether you have small children, or work shifts, it is well worth finding twenty minutes of each day to call your own. If you can manage to do this, you will be more able to give yourself more fully to whatever you have to do next, whether it's meeting a deadline, chairing a meeting, negotiating a deal, collecting the kids from school, or hosting a dinner.

UNTIL YOU VALUE YOURSELF, YOU WON'T VALUE YOUR TIME. UNTIL YOU VALUE YOUR TIME, YOU WILL NOT DO ANYTHING ABOUT IT.

M. Scott Peck

Giving yourself permission

There is a reason why the lure of sleep can sometimes feel very strong—irresistible, overwhelming, seductive. Sleep is good for you, and making it pleasurable is nature's way of trying to ensure that we do it regularly. The trouble with today's society is that the Puritan ethic rules: taking time for ourselves is something we find difficult. Taking time for ourselves that feels good? Almost impossible! Which is strange, because if it is good for our health, and if nature insists we need to do it—like eating our greens—we should.

Taking time

It sometimes feels impossible to find, or make, time to rest when schedules are very busy. At this point it's important to realize that taking a little time for yourself, such as halfway through the day, will pay dividends throughout the remainder of the day. Whatever tasks you have ahead of you will be accomplished more efficiently and, just as important, with less wear and tear on yourself. It's a false economy not to be strict about grabbing time for yourself every day.

It's not always easy to do this when you are on someone else's time sheet, but you are entitled to a break. Try not to use this time to do extra work, catch up, or rush around. Stop work while you eat your lunch, and eat out at a café, or in a park when the weather's good. Go for a short walk. Find somewhere quiet to read a little, or listen to some music on a personal tape or MP3 player. Then stop for a while, close your eyes and drift off for ten minutes.

Finding quiet

Although it's not imperative to have silence in which to rest, some low-key music you're particularly attuned to can help reduce the time it takes you to switch off and chill out. It is usually helpful to escape from the sort of background noise that would distract you. Switch the telephone over to the answer machine. Turn off the news on the radio. If your open-plan office is constantly buzzing, find a quiet corner elsewhere—leave the building if you have to.

Getting comfortable

First of all, you have to get comfortable with the idea that you're entitled to time out. Then you have to get physically comfortable to take some time out!

The best position for napping is lying down, with back and neck adequately supported. If you work from home you can use your bed or hit the couch. A comfortable chair, with your feet up, is the next best. Things are different if you work in an office. If you have your own office, and your chair is comfortable, use this, together with a neck cushion.

Take the telephone off the hook, and switch off your cellphone and pager. Put a note on the door saying "Do Not Disturb"—it's unlikely that anyone will need anything urgent for twenty minutes, and it won't hurt them to wait. For all they know, you are preparing the next sales forecast uninterrupted! If all else fails, keep a small pillow in your drawer, and rest your head on your desk. Whatever your circumstances, you are entitled to this time out, and will perform better as a consequence.

YOU MUST SLEEP SOMETIME BETWEEN LUNCH AND DINNER, AND NO HALFWAY MEASURES. TAKE OFF YOUR CLOTHES AND GET INTO BED. THAT'S WHAT I ALWAYS DO. DON'T THINK YOU WILL BE DOING LESS WORK BECAUSE YOU SLEEP DURING THE DAY. THAT'S A FOOLISH NOTION HELD BY PEOPLE WHO HAVE NO IMAGINATIONS. YOU WILL BE ABLE TO ACCOMPLISH MORE. YOU GET TWO DAYS IN ONE—WELL, AT LEAST ONE AND A HALF.

Winston Churchill

Feng shui

Feng shui is the Asian practice of utilizing the energy of a home in a way that works best with the resident's personal energy. The idea is that when these energies are in harmony, the individual benefits not only in terms of health and wellbeing, but also in terms of happiness and success.

The direction in which the body faces during sleep is considered important. Sleeping with your head pointing east is thought to be beneficial for those trying to build their own career or business. A northeast position provides a more competitive, motivating, and sharper energy. A northwest position is the classic position for leadership. If you want more romance and pleasure in your life, opt for a sleeping position with your head pointing west. A southwest position tends to make people more cautious, especially in their business dealings, and it isn't recommended for anyone concerned about their health. Sleeping with your head pointing south is ideal for promoting passion, intelligence and even fame. This option can cause sleeplessness, though, as it represents the middle of the day—not considered the optimum time for sleeping, unless you're taking a nap! A southeast position is also good for positive developments in business or work, but at a gentler rate of progress.

Building on this basic information, you can combine different positional energies, depending on what you would like to achieve—for example, by napping in a room in the east part of a house, but with your head facing north. Although, if you nap in a southern room, pointing south, you may find dropping off difficult!

With this basic knowledge of feng shui, you can thus make your time out even more effective, by choosing which way you lie when you nap. Additional feng shui considerations include not sleeping opposite a mirror: it is believed that when we sleep our bodies emit energy, as part of a cleansing process, but this won't work with a mirror opposite because it will reflect the energy back.

Charles Dickens

Charles Dickens always ensured he slept with his head pointing north, and when away from home he carried a compass to check—which must have made him a very tiresome house guest if the beds needed rearranging! This, however, is an ideal position for restorative sleep. Letting your own energy be influenced by the energy of the north can make your life more quiet and peaceful.

Spring napping

Spring is a time of new life and vitality. If we are in tune with the seasons, we feel the effect of spring—wanting to start new projects, begin journeys, and inject energy back into our lives after the sluggishness of winter. The lengthening days and increased daylight, combined with sunshine in clear skies, and bright light without the inertia produced by intense heat, all help encourage activity.

But this should also be a time of pacing ourselves, of not over-extending our energy and burning out. The year is still young, and like the young, we need to take regular time to recharge—the nap remains essential. However, whereas we may have napped in the late afternoon in winter, we may need to take our nap a little earlier to restore our energy after the activity of the morning.

Summer napping

After the first burst of spring, summer has a different energy. In traditional Chinese medicine, yin and yang are the two life forces. Yang represents heat, light, sun, and outward movement. While spring is associated with a young yang, summer has a more mature yang. Summer yang is gentler than that of spring, and linked with

wisdom, strength, and taking time a little slower. This fits in with what in the northern hemisphere is a time of greater heat, when daytime physical effort is ideally restricted to hours when the air is cooler, and rest is appropriate when it's too hot for activity. Unsurprisingly, this is why the siesta was born.

Fall napping

Many find the first, crisp days of fall invigorating after the summer's heat and respond with renewed activity and energy, in a similar way to their reaction to spring. Yet at this time we are also beginning to withdraw, and to be reflective about the year's activity. Napping in the fall can often have an edge of wistfullness, melancholy, and contemplation. There's a particular rich smell of leaf mold in the air, which marks the change in season. It's as if we are preparing for and adapting to a slower rhythm. We may be more focused toward consolidation of energy, concentrating and conserving it rather than expanding outward, despite the galvanizing effect of the crisper weather.

Winter napping

As the year draws to its close, we may need our naps not so much to restore activity, but to process thoughts. The longer, darker days can be quite depressing for a lot of people, who try to compensate for the lack of light by pushing themselves harder. They may feel that napping is counterproductive, but it remains just as necessary even if its focus is different. Grabbing some daylight, with at least a regular walk outside, can help banish winter blues, and make a nap indoors feel less sluggish. Napping in front of a fire, watching the flames and listening to the gentle hissing of burning logs, is soporific in the extreme.

3

THERE IS A TIME FOR MANY
WORDS, THERE IS ALSO A
TIME FOR SLEEP.

Homer

Naps for all reasons

The essential nap

Are you persuaded yet of the essential nature of the nap? Then you must schedule in a period of twenty minutes a day, every day, that allows for this possibility. Make it an essential part of your daily allocation of time, then fix it for roughly the same time each day, until it becomes automatic. Create a small ritual around it. Make a cup of camomile tea, put on the slow movement of a piano concerto, lie on the couch, close your eyes and rest; by the time you reconnect with the world, your tea will be the right temperature to drink.

You, yourself, as much as anybody in the entire universe, deserve your love and affection.

Buddha

The opportunistic nap

This is the nap that you take when you get an unexpected opportunity. A meeting has been deferred, a flight delayed, you've arrived twenty minutes early to pick up the kids…. OK, so you could make a list of groceries, you could check that report, but you could also take the time to chill, to disconnect from the world for a while and replenish your energy.

It is unlikely that you will have anything with you to make your nap more accessible, but find the quietest corner you can where you can rest your head without interruption, or, if you are in the car, lock the doors and tilt the seat back, make yourself comfortable, close your eyes and run through the breathing exercises that should help you drift off.

Even if you only manage to phase out for a while, rather than actually drop off, because of the unfamiliarity of your surroundings, be reassured that the benefit is there. Taking the pressure off yourself, in the middle of a busy day, is well worth the attempt as the rewards are great.

The executive nap

You may be the first executive in your company to integrate a nap into your daily schedule, but you certainly won't be the last. Senior managers may fear this will set a precedent, so reassure them that it will, but only for the good of the company. You will work much more effectively afterwards. Forget the ethos of presenteeism; you will be the one working effectively at 6 p.m. when the others are struggling to finish on time.

In the US, the National Sleep Foundation surveyed a variety of workplaces throughout the country and found that 16 percent of these provided places where employees could actually nap at work! Although a small proportion, it is not insignificant, and figures suggests it's a growing trend.

Turn your chair back to the door, drop the blinds, and if necessary put up a sign saying "Meeting in Progress." Switch the telephone to silent and the answer machine on and, if the office tends toward noise, use headphones to listen to some gentle, rhythmic and quiet music. Choose something very familiar so it doesn't stimulate your brain.

Bill Clinton

United States President Bill Clinton was renowned for taking daytime naps whenever he could. Given the amount of traveling that a head of state does today, learning to nap on Airforce One, or in the quiet of the Oval Office, was very much to his advantage; jet lag is not really an option when you are President of the United States.

The discerning nap

However much you love the company of your family and friends, taking time out from the stimulation of their company helps to reinvigorate your relationships with them. Think how many men you know who retire to "read the newspaper" after a meal, a euphemism for a nap if ever there was one!

If you are discerning about the use of your time, allocating some for yourself, you will find that others will respect you for it. You don't have to absent yourself for long, or take yourself far away—the gentle background of domestic life can be quite conducive to napping. So make your excuses, take yourself off, and enjoy your nap knowing everyone will benefit.

Ensure you have those items close by that will facilitate your nap: a soft blanket, a neck cushion, a sandalwood incense stick, whatever you need to make the time truly yours.

I LOVE TO BE ALONE. I NEVER FOUND A COMPANION THAT WAS SO COMPANIONABLE AS SOLITUDE.

Henry David Thoreau

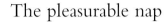

The pleasurable nap

This is the nap that needs no excuses. This is for the sheer pleasure of closing the door on the world, slipping off your shoes, putting your feet up and sipping a delicately flavored jasmine blossom tea.

Take the time to go through the morning's events, deliberately listing those things that have given you pleasure, however small. A smile from the postman, the driver who acknowledged you with a cheery wave when you let him into the traffic, the fresh flowers on display outside the florist's, the blackbirds singing on the lawn, the new buds in the hedgerow. Once you start noticing the good things, you have less time for the negative, and this lifts your mood, banishes worries, and makes it easier to nap, infused with a warm feeling of pleasure.

The healing nap

There is one occasion, above all, when the nap's efficacy should be respected, and this is when you are recovering from illness. The body has a remarkable self-healing ability, but it needs your help. Whether you are recovering from a major illness, injury, or just the flu, give your body the rest it needs to do the healing required.

You may be encouraged to do a little more each day of your convalescence, but this should be balanced with rest. Create a nap ritual, as part of your healing, for this purpose every day. Light an incense burner with oil of lavender to infuse the air, ensure your feet are warm—keep some cashmere socks on the radiator and slip them on before you rest—and make a cup of echinacea tea sweetened with manuka honey, with a slice of lemon.

Keep the light gentle, use a violet-colored lightbulb, or have an amethyst healing crystal close by. Go through the breathing exercises (see page 32) to ensure that the oxygen your body needs to revitalize it is available. Allow your mind to drift through images of good health and vitality. Not only will your rested body improve faster, but the positive effects of auto-suggestion—Emile Coué, the father of auto-suggestion, advocated repeating the words, "Every day, in every way, I am getting better and better" for good effect—can be beneficial while your mind is in this resting state. Try it, and you'll find it helps restore your health.

KNOWING THAT NAPS ARE GREAT FOR YOUR HEART ALLOWS ME TO LIE DOWN WITHOUT GUILT.

Gail McMeekin

The scented nap

The part of the brain responsible for smell is close to the limbic center, responsible for emotion and memory. The benefit of this is that through smell we can activate pleasant and restorative memories. Deep within the limbic system is the amygdala, one of the most primitive parts of the brain, but very important because it is considered to be the brain's pleasure center.

Accessing and activating this area can be done through smell, and you can create your own scent memories by using particular scents that you associate with time out, relaxation, and napping. In time, just a whiff of the scent will become associated with pleasure.

So, before taking a nap, massage your hands with a little almond oil, to which you have added a couple of drops of a favorite essential oil—something subtle, such as rose, neroli, or ylang ylang, for example. Then, not only will the scent become associated with relaxation, but this will also be reinforced by the pleasurable physical sensation of massaging your hands. Of course, if you can get someone to do this for you sometimes—and your feet, as well—before you nap, so much the better!

Napoleon Bonaparte
Famed for his ability to manage with little sleep, Napoleon took naps whenever he could and had the fortunate knack of being able to nap easily. He also said that a hot bath was worth four hours' sleep—my guess is that he napped in the bath as well.

The baby nap

This is recommended for all new mothers: when your baby naps, grab the time for yourself. Don't use it to catch up with chores; they can wait. Take the telephone off the hook, play some gentle music, and make this a special time for you.

You need your rest to provide the care your baby needs, especially if your nights are still interrupted. Producing breast milk takes extra energy too, and many breastfeeding mothers find they automatically take a nap, if they are lying or sitting with their feet up, while they feed. And what could be nicer than to bond with your baby in this way? Use the time, to get to know your baby and to recharge your maternal batteries.

There never was a child so lovely but his mother was glad to see him asleep.

Ralph Waldo Emerson

The sensuous nap

This is the nap when you take comfort in the physical sensation of being cocooned in a soft cashmere blanket, resting your head on a silk-covered cushion, while the scent of freshly cut lilac, warmed by the sunlight, drifts across the room. This is the nap that is taken after a restorative bath, the water softened by bath oil scented with a few drops of clary sage, to warm and relax you. This is the nap when you have picked and cut fresh mint for your tisane and sipped it before snoozing. This is the nap when you have done all of the above, and listened to a Chopin nocturne while you did so.

Create your own sensuous haven by combining pleasures to delight all your senses—touch, taste, sight, smell, and hearing. The combination of these is completely individual and can vary, but the aim remains the same—drift off to sleep feeling physically at one with your surroundings. This nap requires a certain amount of forethought and organization.

Touch is as essential as sunlight.

Diane Ackerman

The luxury nap

A nap is a small treat, but an essential one. Its effects are cumulative, and the payback is multiplied. A luxury nap is this essential writ large. Often a luxury nap is taken on holiday. Many people think that being on holiday dispenses with the need for a nap, but this is not so—the benefits of time off from the routine of daily life, on holiday, or at the weekend, can be amplified through the inclusion of a nap. The nap can take on a different quality when you know it will not be curtailed by your usual activities.

If you are away on holiday, you will not be in your usual nap surroundings, so ensure you have with you some items that create nap possibilities—a small herb-filled cushion, some lemon verbena tea bags, a favorite wrap. Much like a child's comfort blanket, familiar items can provide the prompts for relaxation. The luxury nap includes many aspects of the sensuous nap.

This is the nap that includes time for reading beforehand, time for contemplation when you wake again. It's also a nap that can be shared with another—and who knows what other relaxing activity it may lead to?

One of the secrets of a happy life is continuous small treats.

Iris Murdoch

Rest is not idleness, and to lie sometimes on the grass on a summer day listening to the murmur of water, or watching the clouds float across the sky, is hardly a waste of time.

Sir J. Lubbock

NO DAY IS SO BAD IT CAN'T BE
FIXED WITH A NAP.

Carrie Snow

4

Nap necessities

Herbs for napping

The practice of herbalism involves the use of the whole plant to benefit from its therapeutic or medicinal properties. This can make it extremely potent if concentrated. However, herbs can be used in a variety of ways, harnessing the power of their scent, or by making a tisane, or a tincture, or just through adding the herb to the diet. Lettuce, for example, as well as cleansing the palate, is believed to have a soporific effect—witness what happened to the Flopsy Bunnies in Beatrix Potter's story, after they had gorged on the lettuce in Mr. McGregor's garden!

Some herbs are used very specifically for herbal medicine, or phytotherapy, such as St John's Wort for the treatment of depression. Others can have their essence distilled into an elixir, as with the Bach Flower Remedies, which are thought to influence mood and alleviate emotional distress.

However, there are a number of herbs that can be easily accessed and utilized to encourage and facilitate napping.

Lavender *Lavandula augustifolia*
Of all the plants associated with a calming effect, lavender is probably the best known and best loved. It is a small, bush-like shrub, the flowers and leaves of which are both scented, although the scent is more concentrated in the flowers. Once gathered, the flowers can be processed to extract their essential oil, or dried and used in infusions.

Lavender tea can be made by infusing $^{1}/_{16}$oz (2–3g) dried lavender in boiling water, enough for two cups, depending on the strength you like it. Leave to stand for five to ten minutes, then drain. A cup before a nap will help relax you.

Alternatively, many people find a small pillow stuffed with lavender—like a large lavender bag—useful for resting on when napping. Or simply keep a bunch of dried lavender nearby, as you would a potted plant.

Hop *Hummulus lupulus*

Hops are most well known for the role they play in the brewing of beer. The plant grows wild at altitudes of up to 4,921ft (1,500m) in the hedgerows of Europe, and is easy to grow in your garden. Either take a cutting or buy a small plant and include it in the garden.

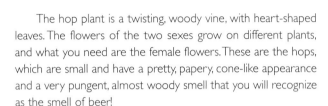

The hop plant is a twisting, woody vine, with heart-shaped leaves. The flowers of the two sexes grow on different plants, and what you need are the female flowers. These are the hops, which are small and have a pretty, papery, cone-like appearance and a very pungent, almost woody smell that you will recognize as the smell of beer!

Hops should be ready to pick in the fall, and can be dried for storage. They have a slightly bitter but aromatic taste and can be used in an infusion (add a little honey to sweeten the taste) of $1/8$oz (5g) of hops to $1^3/4$ pints (1 liter) of boiling water, then drunk warm or cold, as a calming tea before napping.

Another use for hops is to double the quantity in $1^3/4$ pints (1 liter) of boiling water, leave to infuse for up to ten minutes, and then add to a bath. Hops are not recommended for those with a tendency toward depression, or pregnant and breastfeeding mothers. Some people experience an adverse, allergic reaction to hops.

Lemon balm *Melissa officinalis*
Lemon balm grows rampant in many gardens once it has been sown. Its thick, dark green, slightly hairy leaves are reminiscent of nettles, another herb, but these plants are benign. The flowers are white or pinkish and grow at the point where the leaves meet the stem, flowering between July and September.

This plant has the most wonderful, soft lemony scent when its leaves are crushed. The smell alone can lift your mood, but the plant's medicinal properties mean that it is recommended for nervousness and mild depression. For this use, the leaves are dried and powdered and put into capsules to take. It is possible to extract the essential oil of lemon balm, but it is a low-yielding plant, which makes it one of the more expensive varieties to buy, although a little goes a long way.

The easiest way to use it is to pick it and have it fresh in a vase near where you nap, or dry it and add it to a herbal pillow.

The only note of caution is that lemon balm shouldn't be used continuously over a long period of time (no longer than one month), as it may reduce hormonal activity in the sex glands. And it shouldn't be used by couples trying to conceive.

NAP NECESSITIES

Camomile *Matricaria recutita* **and** *Chamaemelum nobile*

After lavender, camomile is probably the herb best known for its soothing qualities. It has a small, daisy-like flower and lanky stems with little, jagged-edged leaves. The whole plant exudes a pleasant, subtle scent, and one variety is chosen instead of grass to create a lawn that is wonderfully relaxing to nap on during a warm summer's day.

The flowers of camomile are collected soon after the buds begin to open and can be used fresh, but they have a greater potency if allowed to dry. They can be stored in a cool, dark place for up to a year.

A tea, or tisane, can be made using camomile flowers, and it is a good choice after a meal because of its digestive effect. For this reason it is often recommended, in diluted form, for restless babies who may have colic. It is also possible to extract the essential oil of the camomile plant, but again it is a low-yield plant so this tends to be expensive.

Make your own herb pillow

This needn't be large—just 12 x 6in (30 x 15cm) is adequate. Choose a soft, loosely woven cotton for an inner lining, then a similar natural fabric (silk is nice) for the outer covering (which can be removed and washed). Select one or all of the herbs outlined on pages 67–70, dried, to include in whichever proportions please you. After a while the contents will lose their scent and potency, but they can easily be replaced.

Foods for napping

Choosing carefully what you eat at lunchtime can both help you nap and help your energy levels afterward. Primarily, you need to include both protein and carbohydrate at lunchtime. Carbohydrate has a role in supplying what the brain needs for production of the feel-good hormone, serotonin. A depressed brain finds it harder to sleep, and also harder to wake cheerfully. Protein is important, too, to keep a check on blood glucose levels as well as nourish the body's cells.

While a warm, milky drink is recommended before bedtime sleep, it isn't necessary for napping. You would be wise, though, to avoid stimulating caffeine-heavy drinks, such as coffee, tea, and colas and opt for freshly brewed herb teas instead.

Lettuce is known to be soporific, because it contains an opium-like substance called latucin, as well as being high in magnesium, which is a stress-reducing mineral. When it comes to fruit, bananas are your first choice: they contain tryptophan, which helps in the production of serotonin, plus the stress-reducing vitamin B6. Oatmeal contains a substance called gamma-amino butyric acid, or GABA, which plays a vital role in mental relaxation; it may seem an odd choice for lunch, but you could make your own low-sugar flapjacks.

Other foods to add to the list include pumpkin seeds, seaweed, sweet potatoes, globe artichokes, avocados, tuna, turkey, tofu, yogurt, almonds, peaches, millet, cottage cheese, potatoes, dates, sunflower seeds, and mushrooms. What you are looking for are foods that provide good quantities of B vitamins, magnesium, calcium, and vitamin C (needed to convert tryptophan to serotonin), all of which helps to calm and nurture your brain.

Perhaps a prime example of a soporific meal is a Mediterranean one: pasta followed by salad, dressed in olive oil. Pasta has the added advantage of being a slow-release carbohydrate compared with white bread or potatoes, so will help maintain your energy levels throughout the afternoon. All of which could go some way to explain why southern Europeans are accustomed to taking a nap after lunch, and then working again into the evening.

Thomas Edison

Edison, who was the holder of 1,093 patents including the electric lightbulb, was notorious for working on his projects nonstop for up to five days at a time, round the clock, taking only short naps. He also claimed that he slept only four hours a night, which is likely, but he also napped.

One of his patrons, Henry Ford, arrived unexpectedly at Edison's office one day and was told not to disturb him, as he was napping! He tended to take one to two naps a day on average and they usually lasted between one and two hours. So he was, in fact, averaging around seven to eight hours' sleep altogether in twenty-four hours.

FOR MYSELF I NEVER FOUND NEED OF MORE
THAN FOUR OR FIVE HOURS' SLEEP IN THE
TWENTY–FOUR. I NEVER DREAM. IT'S REAL SLEEP.
WHEN BY CHANCE I HAVE TAKEN MORE I WAKE
DULL AND INDOLENT. WE ARE ALWAYS HEARING
PEOPLE TALK ABOUT "LOSS OF SLEEP" AS A
CALAMITY. THEY BETTER CALL IT LOSS OF TIME,
VITALITY, AND OPPORTUNITIES.

Thomas Edison

Colors to nap by

According to ancient Hindu wisdom, the chakras, seven centers of different energies within the body, are thought to be influenced by different colors: the same seven colors that occur in natural form in the rainbow. Each color has a different vibrational energy and that can help stimulate mood changes and physical changes in the body. All colors have positive and negative effects, depending partly on the depth and intensity of color used, and to what effect.

Knowing the benefits of the different colors means you can harness this information to your advantage—either through creating a color haven in which you can rest, painting your bedroom an appropriate color, or using a picture or colored cloth to gaze on. When creating the perfect environment in which to nap, choose an appropriate colored lightbulb as well, and literally bathe in its light.

Rose for tranquility
Blue for relaxation
Green for renewal
Lilac for equilibrium

Red, deep pink, and rose

Associated with motivation, stimulation, activity, warmth, and the circulatory system within the physical body, the color red is linked to blood cells and raises blood pressure. It also helps relieve depression and lethargy. Red is the color of the root or sacral chakra and is needed to provide the energy to balance the other chakras.

Use red when you are tired, cold, and need energy and self-confidence. It is a helpful color when you are starting a cold, but it shouldn't be used if you are feeling out of balance, angry, or have heart problems.

Orange and apricot

The color of creativity, vitality, confidence, and communication, orange also is the color of calcium, so is excellent for nursing mothers, and good for bones, nails, hair, and teeth. Wrapping the lower half of the body in orange helps with constipation and a spastic or sluggish colon. Lighter hues of orange can help relieve the symptoms of arthritis.

These colors are good for beating depression, loneliness, or boredom and are the color of joy. They are linked to the spleen chakra, and help when you lack motivation to work.

Yellow and lemon

Warm sunshine, hope, cheerfulness, and optimism are all associated with the color yellow. It strengthens the nervous system and muscles, helps relieve indigestion, and is an excellent color for inflammatory disorders of joints so can alleviate arthritis. Yellow can also assist in loosening calcium deposits within the system, making it effective in relieving stiffness in the joints.

Avoid too much yellow if you are feeling restless, but draw on it when you are feeling dissatisfied, nervous, or tired. Yellow is linked to the solar plexus chakra, and so to the nervous system.

Green

Green benefits the central nervous system, and is also good for balancing and cell restoration. It promotes the building of muscle, skin, and tissues. Green also relieves tension, as it has a harmonizing effect, and it has sedative properties, too. It is often considered the color of wisdom—as can be guessed from the name of the color sage.

Surrounding yourself with green plants will help to restore balance and harmony in your home or office. Plants provide an energy that is helpful if you need to calm yourself before an important meeting.

Blue

Blue is calming, relaxing, and will reduce all heat within the body. It is soothing for fevers, burns, and sunstroke. It is linked to the throat chakra, so is wonderful for soothing sore throats. Blue promotes serenity and release from tension, and its energy is helpful if you've had a shock.

Use blue when you want to relax before public speaking, or if you have a headache. Working under a blue light can boost your productivity.

Indigo

Linked with the pituitary gland, a vital endocrine organ in the brain that balances hormonal function, indigo is also the healing color for neuralgia and problems associated with eyes, ears, and nose. This color is especially valuable as a blood purifier.

Linked to the "third eye" chakra in the center of the brow, indigo is the color of intuition. It is a useful color when you have trouble sleeping, and it is also good for hearing problems. It has an effect on fine nerve function so helps balance subtle nervous energies, such as fear and frustration.

Violet

This is a powerful color for promoting alertness and change. It increases articulateness, open-mindedness, and expansion of thought and creativity. It is also a very spiritual color and linked to the crown chakra at the top of the head.

On the physical level it helps headaches, swellings, cuts, and bruises and aids in the removal of toxins and congestion from the body. It works wonderfully with the immune system, acting as a protection against invasion by harmful bacteria and viruses, and if you suffer from hay fever, it is beneficial when the pollen count is high.

Essential oils for napping

Our sense of smell is closely linked to the limbic system of the brain, which is the first part of the brain to develop in an embryo. The limbic system plays an unusual role in our emotions and memory, which explains why different smells can evoke powerful memories and have an effect on our emotions. The smell of baking bread, for example, can automatically make us feel cared for because in our minds it is linked to warm kitchens, and someone making sure we will be fed. Freshly mown grass may remind us of a childhood summer while the smell of lavender might evoke the comfort and security of a grandmotherly hug.

You can use this link between particular smells, memory, and positive emotion to your advantage when trying to create a mood for relaxation and napping. Essential oils have much to recommend them here, not least because they have therapeutic properties as well.

Keep a range of your favorites to hand and use them singly in a vaporizer, or in combination in a massage oil. You can use a drop, diluted in a carrier oil, to rub gently on your temples before you nap. If you do these things regularly, you will start to associate a particular essential oil with relaxation, letting go, and napping. It is on a par with a Pavlovian response, and helps shorten the time between a state of alertness and being able to relax enough to nap.

Lavender

One of the all-time favorites, lavender has even been found to reduce the incidence of fits among epilepsy sufferers, so potent an effect can it have on the limbic system. For the rest of us, the calming oil helps balance mind and body, soothes tired muscles, and aids sleep while benefiting the immune system through the induction of feelings of tranquility.

Rose

Rose is both soothing and uplifting and has such a luxurious, feminine scent that it is considered to be a tonic for the female reproductive system. It is wonderful for lifting the mood when feeling tired and sad, for reducing overactivity of the nervous system, and for helping improve fertility.

Camomile

This has a slightly woody smell, and if you have ever lain on a camomile lawn on a summer's day, evoking this state of pleasurable relaxation can be very beneficial. Even if you haven't had this experience, camomile is renowned for encouraging emotional peace and calm, while soothing tired muscles. It is gently calming, and is often used as an aid to sleep, either through massage oil or in a tea. It is so gentle that it is suitable for use with babies.

Geranium

Geranium has strengthening properties so is very restorative to body and mind, while also having a calming effect. It has a sedative but uplifting action on the nervous system and helps to balance stress hormones produced by the adrenal cortex.

Jasmine

Often recommended for women to aid postnatal recovery, this is another very feminine, sensual oil with a lovely uplifting scent. Not only does it have a nurturing effect, it also boosts self-confidence and is emotionally warming.

Ylang ylang

This is a sensual and quite exotic oil—use with care!—from the Malaysian flower of the ylang ylang plant. It also regulates the nervous system while soothing and uplifting the mood, balancing and moderating strong emotions. It is often an ingredient in men's fragrances.

Sandalwood

Considered a relaxing and meditative oil, sandalwood has a 4,000-year sacred history, references having been found in both Chinese and Sanskrit scripts, and it is comprehensively used in Ayurvedic medicine. It also has strong antiseptic properties, but it is generally used for its calming scent.

Neroli

Derived from the blossom of the orange tree, neroli has a delicate, light scent is often used to bring balance in cases of hysteria or shock, as it calms, soothes, and brings feelings of peace. It also benefits nervous dyspepsia.

Grapefruit

Renowned for its ability to refresh and revive, this oil is especially useful when you are feeling low and need to bring some clarity to your thought and vision, as it clears the mind and lifts the spirit. It can also help disperse a headache.

Clary sage

This is a deeply relaxing and mood-enhancing essential oil. It eases feelings of depression and is especially useful when you are feeling exhausted or run-down. Its name is derived from the Latin word, "clarus," meaning "clear," and in medieval times it was used to encourage clear-sightedness.

Music to nap to

Gentle music is well known for its efficacy in calming young children and enabling them to drop off to sleep—so why not use it yourself as part of your nap routine? Not only is it an opportunity to enjoy something soothing that you like the sound of, it can also reduce the distraction of other noises. In addition, listening to music is an active process but one that can override other brain activity and reduce its impact. This can be an advantage when trying to relax.

There is also an emotional element to music. We make connections to sounds that make us feel secure and safe, so if you had a happy childhood and a certain type of music was played a lot, that may be the cue for you.

Finally, the rhythmic quality of music can help promote relaxed brainwaves. Taking this a step further, in research done at the University of Toronto's sleep clinic, recording a sleeping person's brainwaves, and then playing them back to the person when awake, was found to help the subject's insomnia. This "music" doesn't sound much like a conventional lullaby, as it is an audible print-out of the EEG. It doesn't even sound much like music—sometimes it is harmonious, sometimes discordant—but the brain seems to recognize and be influenced by its own sleeping brain music.

Calming music generally has a rhythm that is slower than our heartbeat, at roughly seventy-two beats a minute.

MUSIC MAKES PEOPLE KINDER, GENTLER, MORE STAID AND REASONABLE.

Martin Luther

Not only is this consistent with our own heartbeat, but it is reminiscent of the maternal heartbeat, which created such a sense of security in the womb. If you listen to something with a slow, steady beat, brainwaves begin to synchronize with this rhythm and it can help reduce a beta wave to an alpha wave.

Recent research has also shown that the sound of Tibetan bowls (large metallic bowls that can be made to resonate and hum on striking) produces the same alpha wave pattern as in the brain. Again, listening to such a sound can help create this relaxed and creative state of brainwaves. Specially recorded meditation music often includes these sounds, integrated into music or matched with other natural sounds such as rustling leaves, flowing water, or waves on a beach. For those of us who find turning off difficult, this might be the answer.

Your choice of music for napping should be something you are happy to listen to, rather than merely background noise, and something that has a calming rhythm, but can also be uplifting. We know that when people sing it has an emotional effect and stimulates the production of immune-boosting gamma globulins in the body. To a lesser extent, listening to music can have a similar effect, and if it evokes happy and peaceful memories, so much the better. That way you are using the subliminal effect of the music to your advantage too.

It's useful to be aware that different sound frequencies correspond to different brainwaves; you can use this knowledge to your advantage. For the purpose of a nap, alpha waves are the most effective.

Alpha waves range between 7 and 12 Hz. This is a place of deep relaxation, but not quite meditation. When our brains move from beta to alpha waves, we begin to access the creativity that lies just below our conscious awareness. Alpha waves are on the same frequency as what is known as the Schuman Resonance, the resonant frequency of the earth's electromagnetic field. When our brainwaves are alpha, we are very much in tune with the earth's energy and it makes us feel grounded.

Beta waves range between 13 and 40 Hz. The beta state is associated with maximum concentration, a heightened alertness, and visual acuity. This can be valuable when you are busy working, but extended periods can be exhausting.

Theta waves range between 4 and 7 Hz. Theta characterizes one of the more elusive and extraordinary states of being that is also known as the twilight state, normally only experienced when we drift off to sleep, or begin to surface toward waking. Theta waves produce a sort of waking dream, with vivid flashes of imagery, and it is a state in which we are receptive to information beyond our conscious awareness. Theta waves also provide a gateway to learning and to memory, while theta meditation can increase creativity, enhances learning, reduces stress, and awakens intuition and other extrasensory perceptual skills.

Delta waves range between 0 and 4 Hz and are associated with deep sleep. What's more, certain frequencies in the delta range trigger the release of human growth hormone, which is essential for children's growth and beneficial for healing and regeneration for all of us. This is why deep, restorative sleep is so essential to the healing process. It is not appropriate for daytime naps, though— save it for nighttime.

I think I should have no other mortal wants, if I could always have plenty of music. It seems to infuse strength into my limbs and ideas into my brain. Life seems to go on without effort, when I am filled with music.

George Eliot

Musical suggestions

There is a wonderful variety of natural sounds, either alone or linked to musical compositions including strings, woodwind, harp, or piano, to choose from. Check them out if you want to find something that really will transport you away from the ordinary and mundane, and work toward enhancing the greater possibilities of the nap—those possibilities that enrich your waking thoughts and inspire you.

Cello suites

Cello music is perfect for producing the slow, deep notes that are conducive to relaxation. The sound of the cello seems to resonate with an internal rhythm in the body, influencing and slowing it down. Choose solo cello suites rather than concertos with their variation of slow and faster movements, and orchestral pieces where other instruments intervene. There is a wealth of cello solos to choose from, but the Bach cello suites are good ones to start with.

Gregorian chants

The human voice is a musical instrument unsurpassed in its range and variety, but choose carefully when you want to nap. Chanting male voices can be extremely melodic and also have the benefit of a deep, slow rhythm, especially in a choir. Gregorian chants can seem monotonous to some, but it is this very quality that evokes relaxation, and they were designed to assist a contemplative and meditative state. Research has shown that chanting has a calming, meditative effect on the chanter, as well as on those who listen. Take some time over choosing what works for you.

Piano sonatas

The piano is a versatile instrument, but you don't want syncopated jazz for relaxation—you need melodic and flowing piano music, which is where sonatas come in. You may, however, need to select the adagio movements from your chosen sonata, if the allegro is too pacey for you. Bach wrote the "Goldberg Variations" in 1742, at the request of Count Hermann Karl von Keyserlingk, who had trouble sleeping. And Johannes Brahms was famous for his lullabies!

Spanish guitar

Segovia, the virtuoso Spanish guitar player, has produced numerous recordings that meet the requirements for music to induce napping: melodious, rhythmic, and gentle.

Jazz and blues

This genre has to be carefully chosen and isn't to everyone's taste, but for those of us for whom it works, it can be brilliantly associated with relaxation. Opt for music-only recordings, as once the voice is introduced into jazz it tends to become more stimulating. Composers such as Miles Davies are good.

Harp music

Harp music may not be something you normally listen to, but carefully chosen it can have a very tranquilizing effect. The gentle plucking of the harp strings produces a lyrical and rhythmic sound, not unlike the pattern of alpha waves. It is often included in "new age" compositions, many of which have been specially written to have a calming effect.

Wind chimes

There is something particularly soothing about the discordant but harmonious sound of wind chimes in a gentle breeze, especially if they are wooden chimes with a deeper, more resonant note. In terms of feng shui, wind chimes are considered good news, not so much for the sound they make but because they gently vibrate the air, reenergizing it. If you hang a wind chime near an open door and window, according to the principles of feng shui, it will help cleanse the room as it softly chimes and the sound will break up stagnant air.

Seascape sounds

The deep, melodic rhythms of the sea touch a chord in many people, perhaps because they resonate with the watery sounds heard in the womb, which are buried in our subconscious. Again, recordings of sea sounds are often incorporated into "new age" music, although it is possible to find pure sea sounds if you want to visualize lying on a peaceful beach for your nap.

Whale music, birdsong, and other natural sounds

The "new age" movement has generated a wealth of music to relax by, including whale music, dolphin music, and music specially designed to emulate alpha brainwaves. Some people also find recordings of natural birdsong therapeutic, especially if they grew up in the country and have happy memories associated with it. Rather than the dawn chorus, which is wakeful and slightly discordant, the birdsong of early evening can be easeful. The sound of running water from a stream, waterfall, or fountain (as long as it's gentle and continual) is also soothing. Lapping, not breaking, waves are good too.

MY HEART, WHICH IS SO FULL TO OVERFLOWING, HAS OFTEN BEEN SOLACED AND REFRESHED BY MUSIC WHEN SICK AND WEARY.

Martin Luther

The value of time out

Stop and take a look at your life. If you have picked up this book, it's probably because the idea of a nap is seductive, but when you look at your schedule—there are already not enough hours in the day—you think, how can I make time for a nap?

Now look again at your life. Are you doing too much? Are you trying to do it too fast, with little enjoyment or reflection? Are you allowing any time to simply relax, and do exactly as you would like? If not, you are short-changing yourself, for no good reason: time out is time well spent, and will both improve the quality of your life and probably extend the length of it. No one ever asked to have "I wish I'd spent more time working" engraved on their tombstone. The time to make time for yourself is right now. If you don't do this for yourself, no one will do it for you, and your life will be the poorer for it.

DOLCE FAR NIENTE—*how sweet it is to do nothing!*

A twenty-first century necessity

The other argument for scheduling in time out, as you would any other important aspect of your life, is that it is a necessity to prevent the insidious onslaught of "must-do"—the tyrant of twenty-first century life. "Must-do" soon becomes "must-do-it-now" and the list lengthens and lengthens. So make sure that "must-take-a-nap" is also on your "must-do" list.

How are you going to dream up your best ideas if you never allow time for dreaming? How are you going to have time to reflect on what is good and nurturing about your life if you never stop to consider it? How can you make time for others without making time for yourself first? As we learn more about how our brains work, and the benefits of balance, we should aim towards this, rather than the reverse. So start now!

Picture credits